EXPLORER DETAILS

Explorer's name:	
Street:	
Area:	
City:	
County:	
Region:	
Country:	
Continent:	
Planet:	
Galaxy:	The Milky Way
Galaxy group:	Local Group
...xy supercluster:	Virgo
	The Universe!

ACKNOWLEDGEMENTS

Publishing Director — Piers Pickard
Publisher — Tim Cook
Commissioning Editor — Jen Feroze
Author — Nicola Baxter
Designer — Andy Mansfield
Print Production — Larissa Frost,
Nigel Longuet

Published in April 2017 by Lonely Planet Global Limited
CRN 554153
ISBN 978 1 78657 318 6
www.lonelyplanetkids.com
© Lonely Planet 2017
Printed in China

10 9 8 7 6 5 4 3 2 1

Printed in China

MIX
Paper from
responsible sources
FSC™ C021741

Paper in this book is certified against the
Forest Stewardship Council™ standards.
FSC™ promotes environmentally responsible,
socially beneficial and economically viable
management of the world's forests.

Lonely Planet Offices

Australia
The Malt Store, Level 3, 551 Swanston St, Carlton,
Victoria 3053
T: 03 8379 8000

Ireland
Unit E, Digital Court, The Digital Hub, Rainsford St, Dublin 8

USA
124 Linden St, Oakland, CA 94607
T: 510 250 6400

UK
240 Blackfriars Rd, London SE1 8NW
T: 020 3771 5100

STAY IN TOUCH
lonelyplanet.com/contact

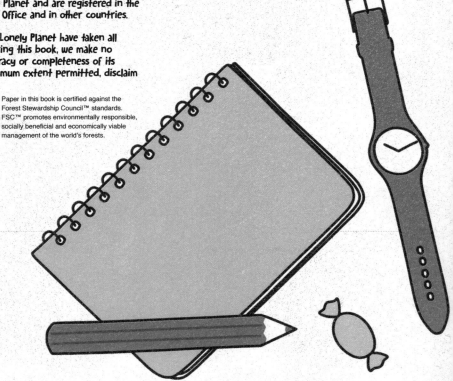

EXPLORER ESSENTIALS

You don't need to trek to the South Pole or hack your way through a rainforest to explore our wonderful world. Your own backyard is just waiting to be discovered.

All explorers know how important it is to make plans. Here's your backyard explorer checklist. Add any extra personal expedition essentials.

- [x] Backyard Explorer book
- [ ] adult mission-base commander
- [ ] suitable clothes
- [ ] shoes for your terrain
- [ ] emergency snacks
- [ ] pens and pencils

- [ ] little bags for specimens
- [ ] fellow explorers
- [ ] watch or phone for timekeeping
- [ ] _____
- [ ] _____
- [ ] _____

A backpack is great for your expedition kit and keeping hands free for investigation.

Steer clear of lions, tigers, hippos, dodgy dogs, helpful strangers, private property, busy roads, crocodile-infested swamps and meteorites.

Mission-base commander's special orders:

!

YOUR VIEW

Start your mission as a backyard explorer by looking out and looking ahead!

LOOK OUT

Fill this space with the view from your window. It could be the window of your room or another room in your home. Show as much detail as you can.

LOOK AHEAD

What would you change, if you could? Draw the view you would like to see and write down your dream plans for the future.

When I am older, I want to live:

because:

MAKE AN ENTRANCE!

Record your own front door here. Add any windows, knobs, locks or signs. Put in any scuffs or scratches. Make it the right colour.

Describe your doorbell's sound if you have one, or what you would like if you don't!

BRRR

DRIING!

DIDDLE-DUM
DIDDLE-DUM
DIDDLE-DUM-DUM
DUM!

DING
DONG!

KALEIDOSCOPE DOORS

Colour these doors to match their labels. Then write on the lines how far you have to go from your own front door to find a front door of that colour.

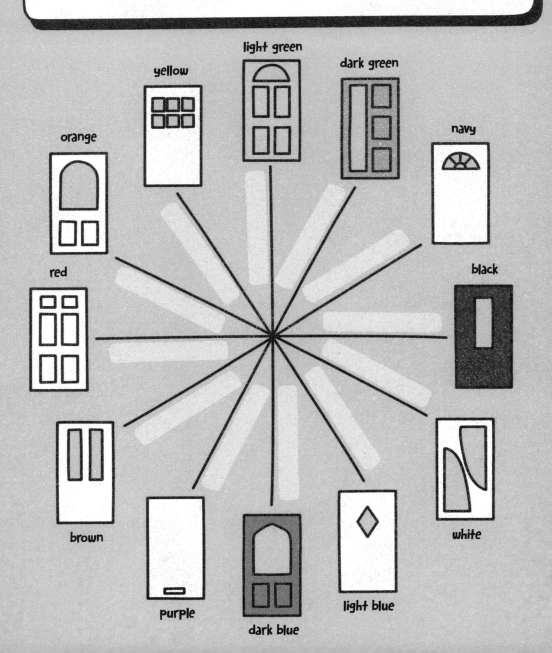

YOU'RE A SPIDER!

Okay, so you don't have eight legs and an interest in plugholes. But you do sit in the middle of a network of places that are important for you.

How far are you from these top hotspots? Add more that you just always need to be near.

School

Best friend

Dentist

Fire station

Doctor

Pool

Hospital

Park

Railway station

Airport

Library

Pizza

HOW WIDE IS YOUR WEB?

Write your name on the creepy critter in the centre. then, all around, mark the positions of the hotspots according to their distances from home. Connect each hotspot with a line to yourself and a line to its neighbour until you have your own wide web for the world you live in.

my home

5 minutes' walk away

15 minutes' walk away

2 miles away

5 miles away

10 miles away

25 miles away

AREA ALPHABET

Get to know your neighbourhood better by filling in this letter-littered lane. How quickly can you find something in your area beginning with each letter of the alphabet?

PLANNING PERMISSION

Is there a horribly hideous building in your neighbourhood? If you had permission to demolish it, what would you put in its place?

Whether it's a mansion just for you or a big public building, you'll have lots of decisions to make. Think about the points below and look around to see what is done in your area. Should your building fit in or be completely different?

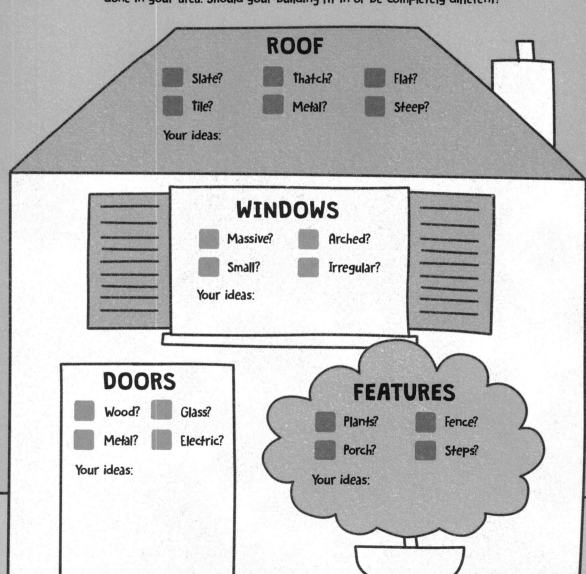

ROOF

- Slate?
- Tile?
- Thatch?
- Metal?
- Flat?
- Steep?

Your ideas:

WINDOWS

- Massive?
- Small?
- Arched?
- Irregular?

Your ideas:

DOORS

- Wood?
- Metal?
- Glass?
- Electric?

Your ideas:

FEATURES

- Plants?
- Porch?
- Fence?
- Steps?

Your ideas:

Now design your dream building. Make sure you give it a name.

FEATHERED FRIENDS

Singing, soaring, spectacular birds can be found around cities and seashores, in fancy fountains and high in the mountains. Everywhere, in fact.

Spot where birds are welcome in your neighbourhood. Make a note of the nearest:

birdfeeder?	bird table?	bird bath?	nesting box?	nature reserve?

Record the birds that visit. Colour the bird blanks to show markings and see if you can find out what they are called.

If you're not sure, name them yourself until you are! Even expert birdwatchers talk about LBJs (little brown jobs) when they're not sure which small brown bird flashed across their view.

BIRD BUNTING

Welcome some chirping chums into your own backyard,
however small it is, by making some bird bunting.

You will need:

- string or thread
- cocktail stick
- foods such as:
  cereal hoops
  grapes
  raisins
  nuts
  blueberries
  popcorn

Simply thread your chosen
treats on to your string,
using a cocktail stick to make
holes if you need to, and
hang the result outside.

Draw your first peckish visitor here.

FACE-TO-FACE

Do you know your neighbours? Are there people you see who seem part of the place, even if you don't know them personally?

Draw some portraits of familiar faces. If you don't know their names, give them working names, such as 'the smiley baker' or 'the lady with the red hat'.

Don't forget to draw the last portrait!

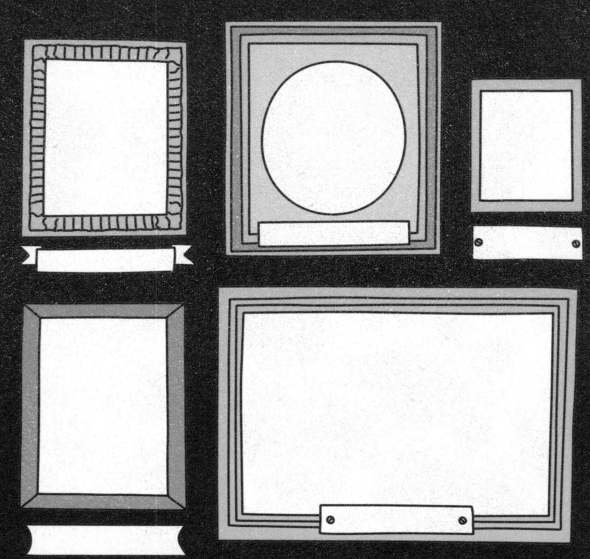

Backyard Explorer

WHAT'S IN A NAME?

Streets and roads sometimes have odd names but mostly they are one of four types.

Fill up these boxes with street names from your area.

Where the road leads

LONDON ROAD

STATION STREET

What is near the road

RIVERSIDE ROAD

CHURCH STREET

A famous person or event

MANDELA STREET

WATERLOO ROAD

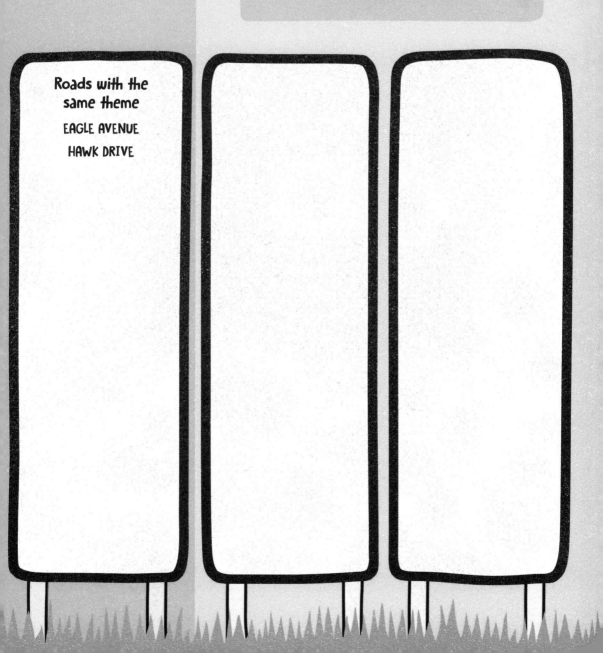

Make up your own categories for neighbourhood road names that don't fit the other boxes.

Roads with the same theme

EAGLE AVENUE

HAWK DRIVE

LEAF FALL

Even big cities have plenty of trees, and the countryside is full of them! Autumn is a good time to collect leaves as they fall but some are evergreen and you will only find a few.

Stick each leaf you find into the book on the shape it best matches. If you can find out its name, write it underneath.

If you collect more leaves than will fit, make a backyard beastie like this one. Why not name it after a local street?

KEEP COUNTING

There are numbers everywhere you look — on doors, road signs, cars, even lamp posts. Here are some games to play during your backyard explorations.

GOING UP, UP, UP

Start at 1 and collect numbers in order. You can spot them on a number plate, a door, a shop, anywhere, but it must just be that number. So '12' must be '12', not part of '3,012'. How far can you go? Keep a note of where you are up to here, so you don't forget.

SPECIAL NUMBERS

Choose a number that is special to you. It could be your lucky number or the day of your birthday or your age. How often can you spot it in your neighbourhood?

My special number:

1.
2.
3.
4.
5.
6.

NUMBER KNOWLEDGE

Did you know that nearly everything on the streets that your local council (or a private company) looks after has a number on it? Can you find a number on any of these? Write them down if you can.

lamp post

road crossing

road sign

traffic light

telegraph pole

bus stop

manhole cover

STREET SMARTS

Your address may give clues to what the street or road you live on is like or used to be like. Do you know addresses in your area that use these words?

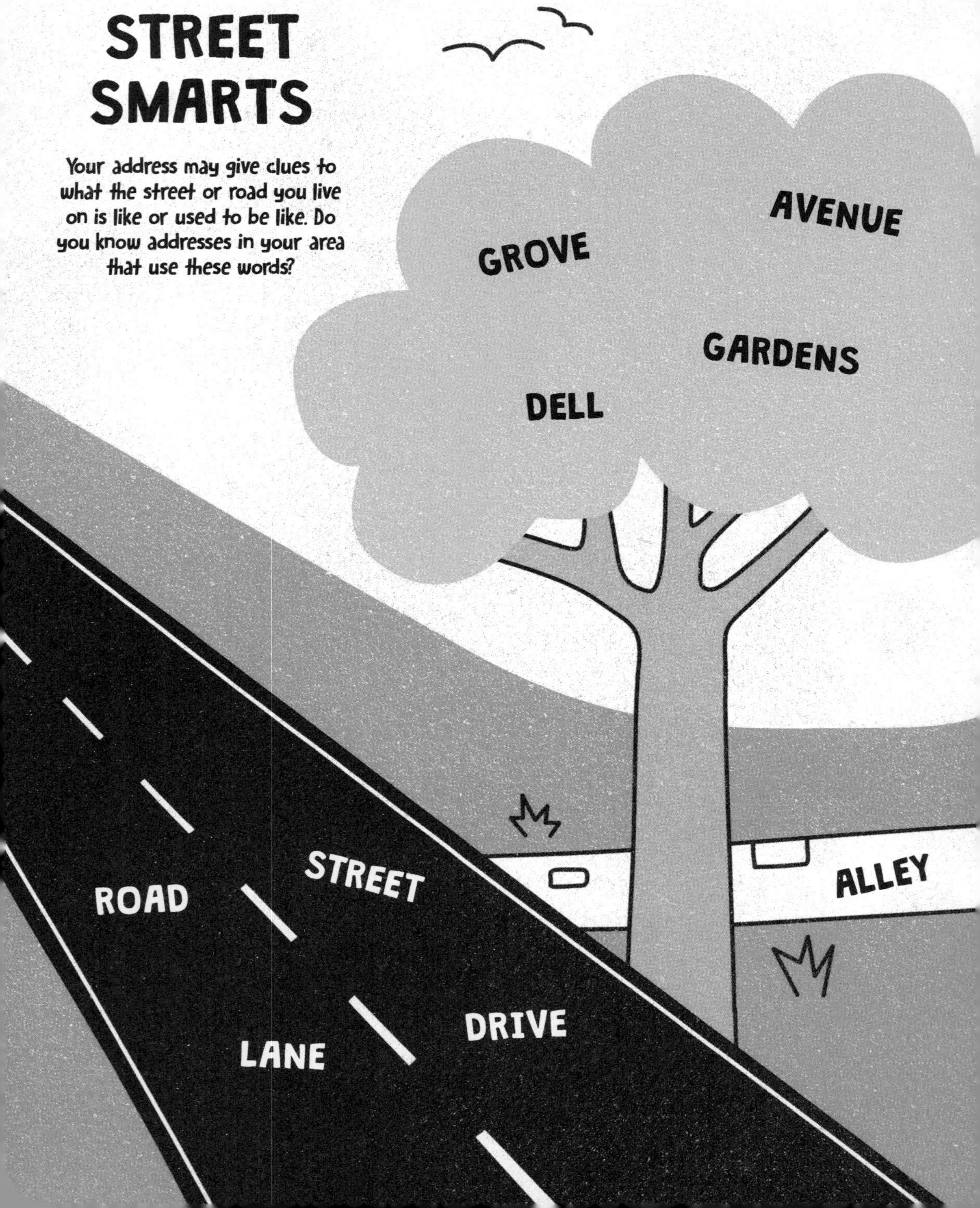

GROVE

AVENUE

GARDENS

DELL

STREET

ALLEY

ROAD

LANE

DRIVE

HILL

RISE

HEIGHTS

VIEW

PLACE   SQUARE

COURT   YARD

WALK   PASSAGE   BRIDGE

As you go out and about, make a list of other words like this here and try to find their meanings. Highlight the one you like best.

MAP MANIAC

Years ago, rich people demolished whole villages because they wanted a quicker route or a prettier view. Suppose you have planning superpowers...

Find, print or draw a map of your area. Cut it up and stick the bits you want to keep on the grid below. Draw in new parts to suit you better.

a mountain to ski down?

a river to run through your garden?

a road straight to a friend's house?

a space for a music festival?

a forest to play in?

Remember to name your new features.

WILDLIFE WATCH

You'll need to be able to sit still and quiet for 15 minutes. Choose a day when you won't freeze or get soaked or suffer sunstroke.

Find a safe place to 'hide'. Inside, looking out of the window would be fine. Or peeping out of a tent, or hidden in some bushes.

Remember, no sudden movements or noises! Pretend you're a tree.

Record all the birds, insects and animals you see in the spaces below and opposite. You can name them, describe them or draw them.

BIRDS

ANIMALS

Keep an eye on the sky for creatures flying over. Watch out for tiny movements among leaves. Pets count, too.

BUGS

Do you know the names of everything you see? Can you find out? Draw the largest creature you spot ... and the tiniest.

LARGEST

TINIEST

SPOT THE DOG

Your neighbourhood is more than a human home. There are sure to be lots of four-footed friends there, too.

Take a look at your area from a pooch's point of view. Where is the nearest:

bin for doggy doo-doos?
_____

water for pets in hot weather?
_____

open space big enough to throw a stick in?
_____

shop selling pet food?
_____

ring to tie a pet outside a shop?
_____

guard-dog warning sign?
_____

Persuade a pet to leave a muddy pawprint here!

puppy-training class?
_____

vet?
_____

IDENTI-KITTY

Make a cat-alogue of famous felines in your neighbourhood.

Use the outlines below to record the markings of cats you see round and about. Fill in what you can about their habits. If you don't know their names, make up a nickname yourself.

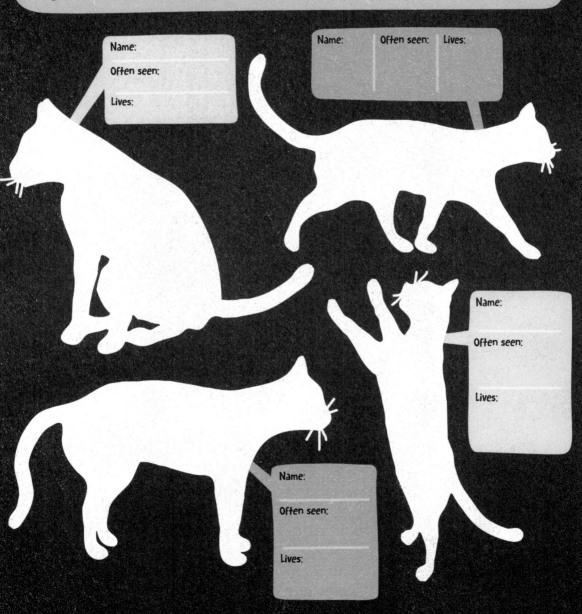

YOUR PLACE'S PERSONALITY

Put away your expert explorer's thinking and find your silly side. Write down the first thing that comes into your head for each of these questions.

1. If your neighbourhood was a make of car, what would it be?

2. If your neighbourhood was a colour, what would it be?

3. A fruit?

4. A single sound?

5. A celebrity?

6. A sporting hero?

7. A movie?

8. A flower?

9. A TV show?

10. A vegetable?

11. A book?

12. An item of clothing?

13. A scent?

14. A chocolate bar?

15. A musical instrument?

Ask a friend to do the same. Do you agree on anything? Or have you both gone loony-list loopy?

PICK IT AND STICK IT

How quickly can you find all these things in your neighbourhood
and tape or glue them in your book?

! Always be careful about picking up objects. Don't touch
anything sharp or dirty and wash your hands afterwards.

1. twig

2. coin

3. seed or berry

4. sweet wrapper

5. bottle top

6. ring pull

7. ticket or receipt

8. dated piece of
newspaper

9. hair bobble or
elastic band

10. feather

time started:

time finished:

PARK PICTURE

Is your nearest park big and beautiful or dull and disappointing? What are its finest features? Write or draw them on the petals of this flower.

Draw the park of your dreams here. It could be a futuristic fantasy or a watery
wonderland. Name it after someone who should be remembered for ever...

BE SENSE—ATIVE!

Eyes, hands, feet — essential for an explorer? Maybe, but as well as sight and touch, try using your other senses.

SHHHH!

Shut your eyes. What can you hear? Capture every sound in the sound waves below. Put nearby sounds — your breathing, perhaps — near the bottom and the furthest sounds near the top.

Is there anywhere in your neighbourhood that is truly silent?

Mark with a letter which sound is:

(A) loudest
(B) quietest
(C) most puzzling
(D) furthest away
(E) most annoying

SMELLY SAFARI

Some animals get loads of information through their noses. Think of dogs and lamp posts! You probably do too, but you don't focus on it.

Take a walk to your local park, school or shops. Walk slowly and stop and write down every whiff on the way. You might smell plants, animals, people cooking, strong aftershave, tarmac in the sun, soil after rain — all sorts of things.

Record your pongy path between the lines.

Home smell =

Smear or spray a safe stinky souvenir here!

Be sensible — no poo or other perilous pongs!

TEXTURE MIXTURE

There are interesting surfaces all around you. How many can you find?

You will need:

- thin paper
- fat wax crayon in a dark colour
- sticky tape or Blu Tack
- scissors

Lay the paper on the surface and rub with the side of a wax crayon to record its pattern.

On a small surface you can hold the paper with your hand. A little tape or Blu Tack can help to hold the paper still on a larger surface.

Cut out small parts of your favourite rubbings and stick them on this gallery page. Remember to record what they are underneath.

THE AWARD GOES TO...

You don't have to live on Mount Everest to be in a record-breaking neighbourhood. Make a note of your area's high spots (and low spots) here.

a round window

fairy lights

BELEIVE

a spelling mistake

1984

a date on a building

a window box

an outdoor fire escape

a poster in a window

a bridge

a satellite dish

a washing line

TRAFFIC TRACK

How busy is the road outside your home?

If you live next to a motorway or on a road with no traffic at all apart from your family, choose another nearby road!

First fill in the grey column with guesses about how many of each traveller will pass your observation station in 30 minutes.

Then settle yourself somewhere safe and find out for real. Colour in a square in the chart for each traveller you see.

If you reach the righthand edge, stop!

		1	2	3	4	5	6	7	8
Walking man									
Walking woman									
Walking child									
Child in buggy									
Dog									
Bicycle									
Scooter									
Motorcycle									
Car									
People carrier									
Bus or coach									
Taxi									
Van									
Truck									
Emergency vehicle									

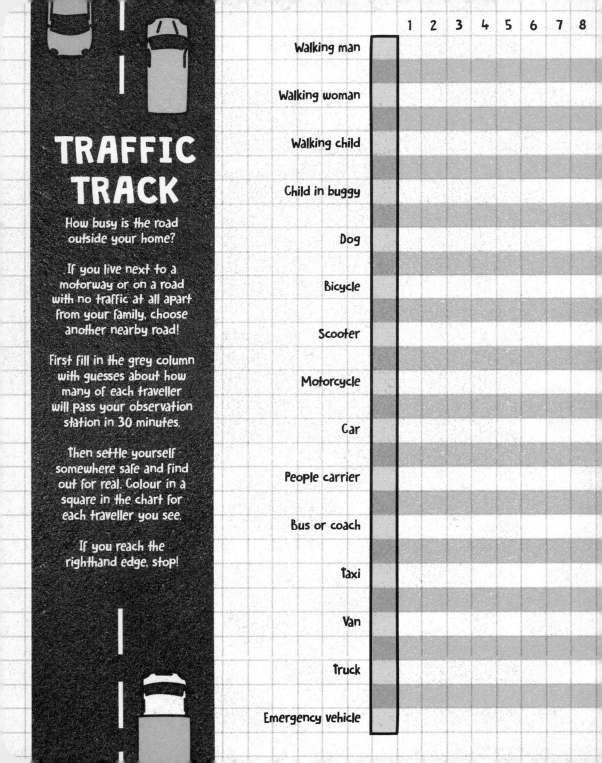

11	12	13	14	15	16	17	18	19	20	21	22	23	24	25	26	27	28	29	30	31	32	33

WEATHER WATCH

Make your own weather station and become a mega meteorologist!

RAIN GAUGE

Make a rain gauge to measure drips or deluges in your neighbourhood at the same time every day.

You will need:
- 2-litre plastic bottle
- scissors
- strong sticky tape
- permanent marker
- ruler
- water

1.

Ask an adult to cut round the bottle just below where the sides become straight.

2.

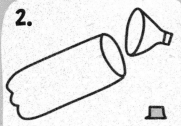

Turn the top part upside down and lodge it in the top of the bottle. Fix it with sticky tape.

3.

Put the ruler beside the bottle and make marks 1cm apart up the side.

4.

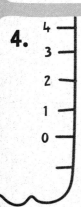

Leave the bottom mark and write '0' beside the second mark, beside the third mark write '1', then '2' beside the fourth mark and so on to the top.

5.

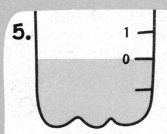

Fill the bottle with water up to the 0. This will stop it falling over in windy weather.

6.

Put the bottle outside in an open spot.

WIND VANE

Find out where your winds are wafting from by recording the wind direction in your neighbourhood every day.

You will need:

- straight drinking straw
- thin card
- scissors
- ruler
- pencil with a rubber on the end
- strong sticky tape
- large, clean yogurt pot with lid
- pencil
- stones or soil
- pin
- compass
- permanent marker

1.

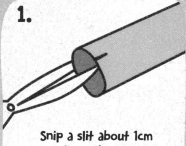

Snip a slit about 1cm long down the straw at opposite sides. Do the same at the other end, making sure the slits line up.

2.

Draw a square with 2cm sides and a square with 3cm sides on card. Cut them out. Then cut the smaller square as shown to make a triangle.

3.

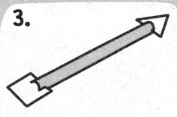

Slip the square and triangle into the slots on the straw to make an arrow, and use sticky tape to fix them in place. Make sure if you lay the arrow down, both ends lie flat.

4.

Fill the yogurt pot with soil or stones so it is too heavy to blow away. Fix the lid on with sticky tape.

5.

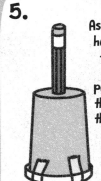

Ask an adult to help you push the pointed end of the pencil through the bottom of the pot, so the rubber end pokes out.

6.

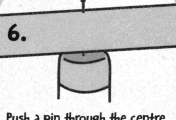

Push a pin through the centre of the straw and into the rubber on the pencil. Your arrow should spin freely. Adjust the position of the pin if one end dips down.

7.

Put the pot outside where it will not be sheltered from the wind. Use the compass to write N, E, S, W on the sides of the pot in the correct positions.

Top tip: the arrow will point to where the wind is coming from. A west wind is blowing from the west.

WEATHER CHART

Keep a record of one month's weather. There is a blank column so that you can measure and add the temperature each day – if possible. If not, add a sad or smiley face to show how the weather made you feel.

Day of the month	Sunny or cloudy	Rainfall (cm)	Wind direction	
1	○			
2	○			
3	○			
4	○			
5	○			
6	○			
7	○			
8	○			
9	○			
10	○			
11	○			
12	○			
13	○			
14	○			
15	○			

Day of the month	Sunny or cloudy	Rainfall (cm)	Wind direction	
16	○			
17	○			
18	○			
19	○			
20	○			
21	○			
22	○			
23	○			
24	○			
25	○			
26	○			
27	○			
28	○			
29	○			
30	○			
31	○			

SUNNY OR CLOUDY SYMBOLS:

Sunny day -☼-   Half sunny, half cloudy day ◐   Cloudy day ⬤

CLOUD CLUES

Scientists have names for different kinds of clouds.

Cirrus

(wispy ones)

Cumulus

(puffy, piled-up ones)

Stratus

(flat sheets)

Finding pictures in clouds isn't very scientific, but it's more fun.
What can you see in these cloud shapes? Draw on some details!

Keep a record of any quirky clouds that float over your backyard.

Did you know?
Nephelococcygia means
'cloud watching' (which
sounds super-scientific!)

STARGAZING

You might think of your neighbourhood as very big or very small. But in space, even our neighbour the Moon is nearly 385,000km away.

From early times, people have seen patterns in the stars. These patterns are called constellations. Do you recognise one of these constellations? First check if you live north of the equator (in the Northern Hemisphere) or south (in the Southern Hemisphere).

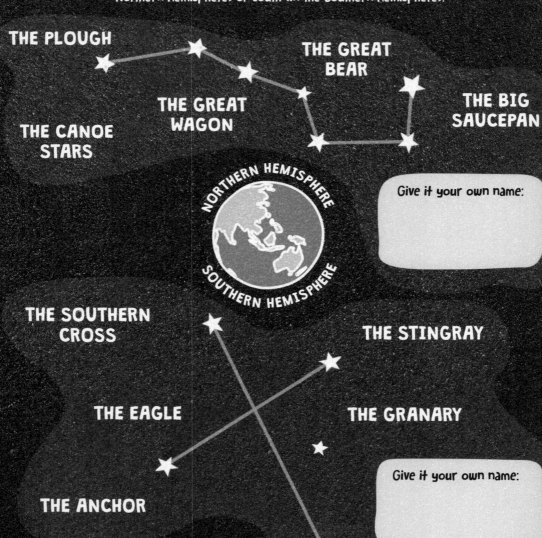

THE PLOUGH

THE GREAT BEAR

THE GREAT WAGON

THE CANOE STARS

THE BIG SAUCEPAN

NORTHERN HEMISPHERE

SOUTHERN HEMISPHERE

Give it your own name:

THE SOUTHERN CROSS

THE STINGRAY

THE EAGLE

THE GRANARY

THE ANCHOR

Give it your own name:

FOLLOW YOUR STAR

Choose a dark night and pick out a star picture in the sky. Don't worry about what other people see. Choose your own. Record its shape by colouring over stars on the grid.

Give your neighbourhood stars their own special name, and that part of the sky will always remind you of home.

NAME:

IS IT A BIRD? IS IT A PLANE?

How busy is your backyard airspace? Choose a fine day to make a flight-path plan.

Lie down outside somewhere safe and comfy with some coloured pens. Watch the sky above your head and draw the path of anything that crosses your view in the blue space below. A bird flying by? A plane zooming high? A flittery, fluttery insect? A floating leaf or feather?

For a flock of birds, grab a fistful of pens and swoop them across the page!

! Don't do this at midday. You should never look straight at the sun.

What drops into your space from above?
Draw the most exciting thing to arrive
from the sky. If it's a feather or a leaf, stick
it on the page. If it's a bird, a meteorite or
an alien, maybe not.

Airborne object landing at:

On:

Thought to be a:

SKYLINE SILHOUETTES

Where does the sky meet your world? On rooftops and chimneys? Trees and hills?

Stand in an open space and draw the skyline you can see in a single line in the boxes below, slowly turning on the spot as you go.

Back at home, colour under your line in a dark colour so that you have a silhouette.
Challenge your friends to work out where you were standing.

TOP TIP:
Why not make a huge version on a roll of
old wallpaper or sheets of newspaper to
go all the way around your room?

Or copy these small
skylines to make
bookmarks or cards.

HOME SOIL

You've looked at the world above your head. Now explore what's under your feet!

SOIL SHADES

What colour is the soil in your area? Which one of these is nearest? Or does it vary? Make up your own descriptions in the spaces. Smear on some wet soil samples.

You don't have to use the colour of foods. Hair colours? Felt–tip pens? Or mix up some paints to match.

Ginger cake

Chocolate cake

Honeycomb

Porridge

RAINBOW ROCKS

What about stones and rocks in your area? All one colour? Lots of different kinds? How many different kinds, colours and shapes can you find in your neighbourhood?

You could collect rocks with holes in them (worn away by smaller stones) and keep them on a string.

You could collect a rock colour-ladder: little pebbles ranging from black to white and all the colours you can find in between.

You might even find a fossil!

What shapes can you make from the stones you've found?

You could look for heart-shaped rocks or rocks that are as near to perfect spheres as you can find.

SOIL SCIENCE

Time to look closer — and it means making a muddy, magic (maybe!) potion.

1. You will need:

- an old spoon
- a large, wide-necked, clear-plastic or glass jar with a lid
- some water

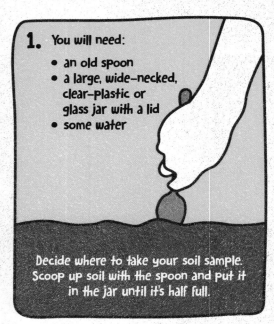

Decide where to take your soil sample. Scoop up soil with the spoon and put it in the jar until it's half full.

2.

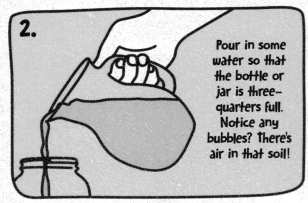

Pour in some water so that the bottle or jar is three-quarters full. Notice any bubbles? There's air in that soil!

3.

Stir your potion really well. Put on the lid and leave the contents for a few hours to settle.

4. When you come back to your jar, the soil will have separated into layers. You could see:

bits of plants (leaves, roots etc)

water (with some stuff dissolved in it now)

clay (grains so small they stick together)

silt (smaller grains than sand)

sand (the largest grains)

stones and pebbles

5. What layers did you find? Draw them on the jar below.
Why not smear some of each layer on the page?
Now compare potions from different places.

Did you find anything
else in your sample?
treasure? Insects?

PAVING PATTERNS

There's more than dirt under your feet. Lots of pavements and open areas are paved with big slabs or smaller bricks. Take a closer look.

Paving is usually made of squares and rectangles of different sizes. Even ordinary concrete slabs can be laid in different ways. Look out for paving like this:

or like this:

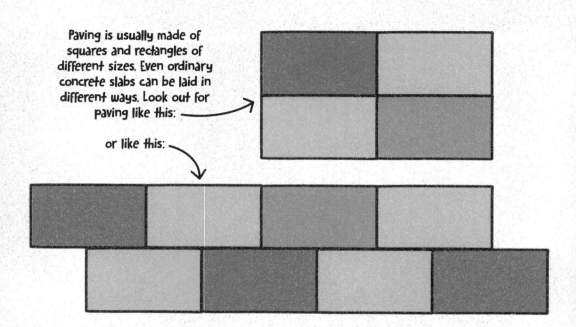

Bricks are rectangles too, usually twice as long as they are wide. They can be laid in even more combinations. Which of these have you seen?

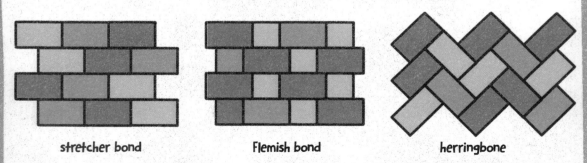

stretcher bond   Flemish bond   herringbone

Record paving patterns you see in your neighbourhood on the grid opposite. Make up some of your own! Add some new paver shapes.

NEIGHBOURHOOD PRIVATE EYE

You know your neck of the woods pretty well by now.
Can you answer these cunning questions? If not, find out!

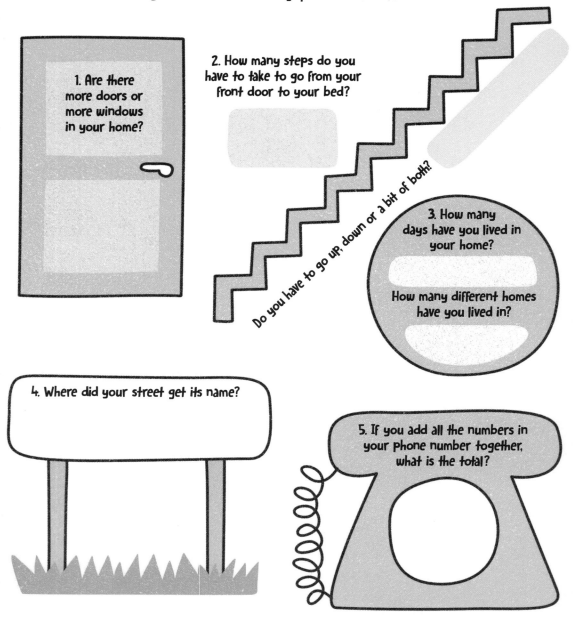

1. Are there more doors or more windows in your home?

2. How many steps do you have to take to go from your front door to your bed?

Do you have to go up, down or a bit of both?

3. How many days have you lived in your home?

How many different homes have you lived in?

4. Where did your street get its name?

5. If you add all the numbers in your phone number together, what is the total?

6. Can you find your way round your home with your eyes shut?

7. What is the furthest you have ever been from home?

When?

8. How close is the nearest street or road with your first name or surname? If there isn't one in the world, which road would you choose to name after yourself?

9. Draw the shape of a local landmark, without looking! How well did you remember?

10. Which is your favourite page in this book?

TIME-AND-PLACE CAPSULE

You've heard of time capsules — collections of objects buried to be dug up even hundreds of years later. Why not make a time-and-place capsule for your own neighbourhood right now? No digging needed!

Fill in the spaces on these pages by drawing, writing or sticking on bits and pieces.

Date completed:

Packaging of your favourite sweet:

Pawprints of pets:

Fingerprints of friends:

Pocket money per week:

three favourite songs EVER:

three best friends:

Front door colour:

Three favourite celebrities:

A pressed flower or leaf:

Trace round your hand on the page.

Who knows where you'll be or what you'll be doing when you look back at these pages sometime in the future, but your time-and-place capsule will bring TODAY rushing back to you.

FEATURING:

WRITTEN BY